Stories from Shakespeare

WITHDRAWN

Level 3

Retold by Anne Collins

Series Editors: Andy Hopkins and Jocelyn Potter

D1043040

Pearson Education Limited
Edinburgh Gate, Harlow,
Essex CM20 2JE, England
and Associated Companies throughout the world.

ISBN-13: 978-0-582-42694-8
ISBN-10: 0-582-42694-4

This edition first published 2000

7 9 10 8

Typeset by Pantek Arts, Maidstone, Kent
Set in 11/14pt Bembo
Printed in China
SWTC/07

Published by Pearson Education Limited in association with
Penguin Books Ltd, both companies being subsidiaries of Pearson Plc

Acknowledgements:
Donald Cooper/Photostage: pp. 6, 11, 44 and 48; Zoë Dominic: p. 20;
Pictorial Press: p. 38; The Ronald Grant Archive: p. 32

For a complete list of titles available in the Penguin Readers series, please write to your local
Pearson Education office or to: Penguin Readers Marketing Department,
Pearson Education, Edinburgh Gate, Harlow, Essex CM20 2JE.

Contents

Introduction

*Then Shylock laughed and said, 'But now let's have a little joke. If you
don't pay me back 3,000 gold pieces at the end of three months, you
must give me a pound of your flesh. I'll cut the flesh from a part of your
body, as I like. Do you agree?'*

Venice was an exciting centre of business in Shakespeare's time.
The rich merchants of Venice bought and sold things from all
the countries round the Mediterranean. *The Merchant of Venice*
tells the story of Antonio, a merchant; his friend Bassanio; the
beautiful and clever Portia, and their friends. It ends happily for
Antonio and Bassanio, but not for Shylock, the moneylender. But
probably nobody in Shakespeare's time liked Shylock or felt sorry
for him.

The Merchant of Venice is one of thirty-seven plays that Shakespeare
wrote between 1591 and 1611. His plays are about many different
subjects. Some are about famous people in history. Other plays are
stories from the literature of his time. Shakespeare took these
stories and wrote new plays around them. Many of his plays take
place outside England – the four in this book, for example, take
place in Venice, Greece, Denmark and Rome.

Not all of Shakespeare's plays end happily. But when people
went to the theatre, they didn't always want plays with happy
endings. They also enjoyed serious plays with sad endings. In two
of the plays in this book – *Hamlet* and *Julius Caesar* – the most
important person dies. The end of their life brings death to many
other people too.

The stories in this book are the stories of four of Shakespeare's
plays. Shakespeare wrote *A Midsummer Night's Dream* at about the

same time as *The Merchant of Venice*. This play ends happily for everyone – the two pairs of lovers, the fairy king and queen, and even the funny workmen from Athens.

People in Britain didn't have a very clear picture of Athens, so Shakespeare could introduce all kinds of interesting people and things in his play – a fairy king and queen, and the juice of a flower with unusual powers. But he also mixed these people with ordinary workmen to make the play funny and more real.

Hamlet is a very serious play; it is Shakespeare's longest play and also one of the most difficult. The part of Hamlet is very difficult to act. Hamlet, the young prince of Denmark, discovers that his uncle murdered his father. He then has a terrible problem. Must he kill his uncle? And what part has his mother, his uncle's new wife, played in her first husband's death? He can't decide what to do.

While he tries to decide, Hamlet brings death to many other people around him. By the end of the play, we feel very sorry for him, but the ending must be a sad one.

Like *Hamlet, Julius Caesar* is a serious play. Shakespeare took the story of *Julius Caesar* from history. But he changed a few things to make it more interesting. The main person in his play is Brutus, an important Roman, not Julius Caesar. Brutus, like Hamlet, has a problem. Will he join the people who are going to kill Caesar? At the end of the play, Brutus dies. The real Brutus died in the same way, and this is the only possible ending to the play. Like Hamlet, Brutus dies bravely. Even his enemy, Mark Antony, says, 'This was the finest Roman of them all.'

William Shakespeare is the most famous writer of plays in the English language, but we know very little about his life. He was born in Stratford-upon-Avon in 1564, in the time of Queen Elizabeth I. His father, John Shakespeare, was quite rich, so William probably went to a good school. In 1582 he married

Anne Hathaway. He was eighteen and she was twenty-six. They had three children – a boy and two girls.

After that, we don't know anything about his life until 1592. At that time, Shakespeare was writing and acting in successful plays in London. We don't know when he went there. But his plays were very popular. By 1597, he was rich and he was able to buy the largest house in Stratford. His last play was *Henry VIII* (1612). The actors at the Globe Theatre in London were acting in this play in 1613 when the theatre caught fire. It was burnt to the ground. Shakespeare died in Stratford on 23rd April 1616 at the age of fifty-two.

The Merchant of Venice

There was a merchant, Antonio, who lived in Venice. Everybody liked Antonio because he was a good man. He had many ships that travelled to other countries. He sold things to people in these other countries, and bought things from them. At the time of our story, Antonio's ships were all at sea.

Antonio had many friends, but his dearest friend was called Bassanio. He loved Bassanio very much. When Bassanio's father died, he left his son a lot of money. But Bassanio soon spent it all; he became poor and very unhappy.

Bassanio was in love with Portia, a lady from Belmont, near Venice. Portia's father died and left her all his money. So Portia was beautiful *and* very rich. Bassanio was sad because he had no money. He knew that many rich young men went to Belmont. They all hoped to marry Portia. So he asked Antonio to lend him 3,000 gold pieces for the journey.

'I haven't any money now,' replied Antonio. 'All my money is with my ships at sea. I'm waiting for them to return.

'But many people here know me and will lend money to me. I'll pay it back when my ships return. Go and find me a money-lender. Then I'll lend the money to you. You can go to Belmont and marry Portia.'

So Bassanio went to a money-lender. This man's name was Shylock.

Shylock had a lot of money, but he loved it too much. He lent money to merchants. But they had to pay him back a lot more money than they borrowed. Antonio didn't like Shylock's way of doing business and Shylock didn't like Antonio either.

'Antonio is kind and will lend his money to everyone,' Shylock thought. 'People only have to pay back what they borrowed. He makes things very difficult for me. And he often tells the other merchants that my way of doing business is wrong. He's my enemy and I can't forgive him.'

Bassanio asked Shylock to lend Antonio 3,000 gold pieces for three months. This made Shylock very happy.

'Now at last I have a way to catch Antonio,' he said to himself. 'I can make things very difficult for him.'

When Shylock met Antonio, he said to him, 'You don't like my way of making money. You've often called me a "dog" in the past. But now you've come to me because you need my help. You want me to lend you money. But what shall I say to you? Does a "dog" have money? Can a "dog" lend a person 3,000 gold pieces? Shall I lend you money because you called me a "dog"?'

But Antonio wasn't afraid of Shylock.

'If you decide to lend me money,' he replied, 'don't lend it to me as a friend. Lend it to me as an enemy. Then if I can't pay you back, you can punish me for it.'

'But I want to be your friend,' said Shylock. 'I want to forget what you've done to me in the past. I'll lend you 3,000 gold pieces and you don't have to pay me back more than that.'

'That's very good of you, Shylock,' said Bassanio.

Then Shylock laughed and said, 'But now let's have a little joke. If you don't pay me back 3,000 gold pieces at the end of three months, you must give me a pound of your flesh. I'll cut the flesh from a part of your body, as I like. Do you agree?'

Antonio thought that this was a good joke. So he laughed and agreed. But Bassanio was afraid and said, 'Please don't agree to this stupid idea of Shylock's. I don't want you to borrow money in this way. Shylock really will do what he says. He really will take your flesh.'

'Don't be afraid,' replied Antonio. 'My ships will return in two months and bring me plenty of money.'

So Antonio borrowed the money from Shylock and gave it to Bassanio.

◆

Before he died, Portia's father made a plan. He wanted to be sure that his daughter found a good husband. 'I'm afraid that a lot of young men will want to marry Portia,' he thought. 'They will choose her because she's rich. So I shall leave three small boxes – a gold one, a silver one and a lead one. To win Portia, the man must choose the right box.'

Later, after her father's death, Portia was sitting with another young lady called Nerissa. Nerissa was a servant, but she was also a good friend of Portia. They were talking about all the young men who wanted to marry Portia. Then another servant came into the room.

'A prince has just arrived from Africa,' he said.

Portia showed the prince the three boxes. The prince carefully read everything that was written on each box.

On the gold box were the words, 'Choose me. You will get what many men want.'

On the silver box were the words, 'Choose me. You will get what you should get.'

And on the lead box were the words, 'Choose me. You must give everything that you have.'

'My picture is inside the right box,' said Portia. 'If you choose it, I am yours. Now choose!'

The prince studied the words on all three boxes again. Finally he said, 'Everybody in the world wants gold and everybody in the world wants Portia. So the gold box is the right box. Yes, I'll choose the gold box.'

Portia gave the prince the key to the gold box and he opened it. But when he saw inside it, he was very surprised. There was a picture of a dead man.

There was also a piece of paper in the box, and these words were written on the paper:

'Many things shine brightly but they are not always gold.'

The prince left with a sad heart. But Portia was very pleased to see him go.

◆

Next a French prince came to Belmont. He was very proud, so he chose the silver box. He read the words, 'Choose me. You will get what you should get.'

'Fine,' said this proud prince, 'I'm a great man, so clearly I should get a beautiful and rich lady like Portia.'

But when he opened the box, he found a picture inside. It was not a picture of Portia, but the head of a stupid man. There was also a piece of paper in the box. It said:

'Many stupid men are covered in silver.'

'I've been stupid too,' said the prince, and went away.

◆

Then a servant came to Portia and said, 'A young man from Venice is on his way here. He wants to try and win you.' This young man was, of course, Bassanio.

When Bassanio arrived, he had many servants with him. One of them was called Gratiano. Gratiano was a servant, but he was also a good friend of Bassanio.

When Portia saw Bassanio, she fell in love with him. Now she became afraid. She didn't want Bassanio to choose the wrong box. So she said to him, 'Please wait a day or two before you choose. If you choose the wrong box, I won't see you again. I can teach you how to choose the right box. But I've promised not to do that.'

'No, I'm too nervous to wait,' answered Bassanio. 'I'll choose now.'

Bassanio studied the words on the gold and silver boxes carefully. He thought, 'The gold and silver boxes seem to promise fine things. But beauty on the outside does not always mean beauty on the inside. The lead box doesn't promise anything. It tells me to give, and to be ready to lose everything. Well, I'm ready to give everything to Portia. So I choose the lead box.'

Portia gave him the key and he opened the lead box. Inside the box was Portia's picture and a piece of paper with these words on it:

'If you're pleased with this, kiss your lady.'

Bassanio was very happy. He turned to Portia and said, 'Dear lady, have I really won you? Will you be mine?'

'Yes, Bassanio,' replied Portia. 'I don't want great things for myself, but for you I'd like to be a thousand times more beautiful and ten thousand times richer. Take me, and everything that belongs to me.'

Portia took a ring off her finger and gave it to Bassanio.

'Take this ring, dear Bassanio,' she said to him. 'When you stop wearing it, that will be the end of our love.'

'I'll die before anyone takes this ring from my finger!' cried Bassanio.

As Portia and Bassanio continued to talk about their love, Nerissa and Gratiano came to them.

Nerissa said, 'We hope that you'll be very happy in your marriage.'

'Yes,' said Gratiano. 'And Nerissa and I have some wonderful news. We're going to get married too.'

As the four happy people were talking about their weddings, a man from Venice arrived with a letter from Antonio. Bassanio opened the letter and began to read it.

While he was reading the letter, Portia looked at Bassanio's face. 'I'm sure that there's very bad news in this letter,' she thought. 'But what's happened?' To Bassanio she said, 'I'm half of you, so I must have half of your problems. Tell me what's in the letter.'

'Well, I'm ready to give everything to Portia. So I choose the lead box.'

'Dearest Portia,' Bassanio replied, 'this letter brings terrible news.' Then he read the letter to her:

Dear Bassanio,

My ships are all lost. Now I have no money, so I cannot pay Shylock. I must give him a pound of my flesh, as we agreed. But if I do that, it will kill me. So please forget about the money that you borrowed from me. I only want to see you now before I die.

Antonio

'You must return to Venice immediately,' said Portia. 'But first let's get married. Then I can give you enough gold to pay Shylock twenty times. When it is paid, bring Antonio back here with you.'

◆

Portia and Bassanio got married, and Nerissa and Gratiano married too. After the weddings, the two men hurried back to Venice.

After they left, Portia thought of a clever way to save Antonio. A good friend of hers was a famous judge. She asked her friend to lend her his judge's clothes and notes. Then she put on the clothes and pretended to be a judge. Nerissa also put on men's clothes and pretended to be the judge's servant.

Then the two women followed their husbands to Venice.

◆

Shylock had a beautiful daughter, Jessica. A good friend of Antonio fell in love with Jessica and ran away with her. Jessica took some of her father's money with her.

So Shylock was very angry with Antonio. He ran angrily through the streets of Venice, shouting loudly about his daughter and his money. Small boys followed him and laughed at him.

When Shylock heard the news about Antonio's ships, he was very pleased.

'Good. Antonio's ships are lost at sea,' he thought. 'Now at last I can kill my enemy.'

He went to see Antonio. A man was just taking him to prison.

'Guard him well,' Shylock said to this man.

'Please, Shylock, I'd like to talk to you,' began Antonio. But Shylock refused to listen.

'Don't speak to me, Antonio,' he said. 'I won't forgive you. You called me a "dog", so now I'll act like a dog. I won't show you any mercy; I'll take my pound of flesh from you.'

'He hates me and he really wants to kill me,' thought Antonio. 'I won't try to speak to him again. I only want one thing now. I want to see Bassanio before I die.'

◆

Antonio was taken to court, and the Duke of Venice took his seat as judge. The duke felt very sorry for Antonio. When Shylock came in, he said, 'Please, Shylock, show mercy.'

'Never,' replied Shylock. 'The pound of flesh is mine by law and I want it. Antonio is my enemy and I hate him.'

'Does everyone kill the things that they hate?' asked Bassanio.

'Don't try to talk to Shylock,' said Antonio sadly. 'He doesn't want to listen. Please be quick and judge me. Give Shylock what he wants.'

'I'll pay you 6,000 gold pieces for the 3,000 that Antonio borrowed,' said Bassanio.

'If you offer me six times that amount of money,' said Shylock, 'I'll still take my pound of flesh. Give me my pound of flesh!'

'How can you hope for mercy for yourself when you show no mercy to Antonio?' asked the duke.

'I'm not afraid. I've done nothing wrong,' said Shylock.

The duke didn't know what to do. Then a young man came

into the room and gave the duke a letter. The young man was really Nerissa. But nobody knew her because she was dressed like a man.

'Sir, a young judge has just arrived from Padua,' she said. 'A friend of yours has sent him to judge Antonio and Shylock. This letter explains everything.'

The duke read the letter and said, 'Ask him to come in.'

The young judge came into the room. It was really Portia, wearing the clothes of a judge. But nobody knew her.

As she sat down, the duke asked, 'Do you know what's happened here?'

'Yes,' said Portia. 'Where are Antonio and Shylock?'

'Here,' said the duke.

Portia looked at the two men. Then she said, 'Shylock has the law of Venice behind him. So he must show mercy to Antonio.'

'Why must I show mercy?' asked Shylock. 'Tell me.'

'Because mercy is a wonderful thing,' replied Portia. 'It falls like soft rain from the sky on to the earth. It brings good things to the person who gives it. Kings have mercy in their hearts, and we should show mercy to other people. So, Shylock, do you still want your pound of flesh?'

'Yes!' answered Shylock. 'I want what is mine by law!'

Then Bassanio said, 'I'll offer Shylock ten times the amount of money that Antonio has borrowed. If this isn't enough for him, please change the law. Please change it and save Antonio.'

'No,' replied Portia. 'If we change one law, then people will want to change other laws. We can't do that.'

'Oh, wise young judge!' cried Shylock.

'Can I see the paper that Antonio signed?' asked Portia. 'I want to see his promise to Shylock – his promise to give Shylock a pound of his flesh.'

Portia read the paper and said, 'Yes, Shylock is right. By law he can take a pound of Antonio's flesh. He can cut the flesh from the place near Antonio's heart. Shylock, show some mercy. Take three times the amount of money. Tell me to destroy this paper.'

'No,' said Shylock, 'I want my pound of flesh.'

'Then Antonio must prepare himself for the knife.'

'Oh, wise young judge!' cried Shylock again.

'Do you want to say anything?' Portia asked Antonio.

'Only a few words,' replied Antonio. 'Bassanio, my dearest friend, goodbye. Don't be sad for me. Tell your wife about me. Tell her how much I loved you. If Shylock cuts deeply, I'll pay him with all my heart.'

'I love my wife very much,' said Bassanio sadly. 'But your life means more to me than my wife and everything in the world. I'll happily lose my wife to save you.'

'It's good that your wife isn't here now,' said Portia.

Then Gratiano said, 'I too love my wife very much. But if it can save Antonio, I'll lose her too.'

When she heard this, Nerissa laughed quietly. 'If you say those things in front of your wife,' she said to Gratiano, 'you'll have a lot of problems at home.'

'Let's hurry!' said Shylock impatiently.

'Take your pound of flesh,' said Portia. 'It's yours by law. This court gives you permission to take it.'

As Shylock moved towards Antonio, Portia spoke again.

'Wait!' she said. 'There's one more thing. In this paper, Antonio promised to give you a pound of his flesh. So you can take a pound of flesh. But there's nothing in the paper about blood. He didn't promise to give you any blood. So if one drop of his blood falls, you'll lose your land and your money.'

'Oh, wise young judge!' cried Gratiano.

'Is that really the law?' asked Shylock.

'Yes,' replied Portia. 'Now you've got what you wanted, Shylock. You've got more than you wanted.'

Shylock was very angry. But he knew that he couldn't win. 'If

'So if one drop of his blood falls, you'll lose your land and your money.'

I cut off a pound of Antonio's flesh, he'll lose a lot of blood,' he thought. 'What shall I do?' Finally he said, 'All right, I'll take the money. Give me three times the amount that Antonio borrowed from me.'

'Here it is!' cried Bassanio happily. 'Take it!'

But Portia stopped him. 'No,' she said. 'Shylock didn't want the money before. He only wanted his pound of flesh.'

'But I've changed my mind,' said Shylock. 'I don't want his flesh now.'

He turned to leave the court.

'Wait, Shylock,' said Portia. 'When someone tries to kill a person from Venice, he must give all his money away. He must give one half of his money to the state of Venice. The other half must go to the person that he tried to kill. And the duke must decide if he lives or not. This is the law. So now you must ask the duke for mercy.'

'Kill me, then,' said Shylock. 'If you take my money, you also take my life.'

'I don't want Shylock's money,' said Antonio. 'But he must promise to leave his money to his daughter, Jessica, and her husband when he dies.'

'Good,' said the duke. 'Do you promise, Shylock? Will you sign this paper?'

'Yes, yes!' said Shylock. 'I'll sign. But please, I must go home now. I'm not well.'

The duke agreed and Shylock left the court.

◆

Antonio and Bassanio were very grateful to Portia. They tried to give her money, but Portia refused to take it.

'Dear sir,' said Bassanio. 'Please take something to remember us. We want to thank you.'

Then Portia had an idea. She decided to play a joke on

Bassanio. So she pretended to notice a ring on his finger. It was the ring that she gave him.

'That's a beautiful ring,' she said. 'Please give it to me. It's the only thing that I want from you.'

Bassanio remembered his promise to Portia about the ring. 'What will Portia say?' he thought. 'She wants me to wear this ring for ever. I can't give it to this young judge.'

'I'll buy you the best ring in Venice,' he said to Portia, 'but I can't give you this ring. It's very special. My wife gave it to me. I mustn't sell it, or give it away, or lose it.'

'I understand,' said Portia. 'You don't want me to have the ring. All right, then. Goodbye!'

She began to walk away.

'Bassanio, please give the judge the ring,' said Antonio. 'He did a lot for us today. He saved my life.'

Bassanio thought about this. He knew that Antonio was right. So he told Gratiano to take the ring to Portia. She was very pleased with it and thanked Gratiano.

Gratiano met Nerissa again. She was still dressed as a man, so he didn't know her. Nerissa decided to play a joke on her husband too. Gratiano also had a ring from his wife. Now Nerissa, too, got this ring back from her husband.

◆

Portia and Nerissa returned to Belmont, and Bassanio and Antonio arrived soon after them.

Bassanio introduced Antonio to Portia and told her about the wise young judge. As they were talking, Nerissa began to cry.

'What's the matter?' Portia asked her.

'Gratiano has given away the ring that I gave him,' replied Nerissa. 'He gave it to a young man.'

'The young man was the servant of the wise young judge,' said Gratiano. 'He was only a boy.'

'You were wrong to give the ring away, Gratiano,' said Portia. 'You promised Nerissa to wear it for ever. I also gave my husband a ring. I know that he'll never give that away.'

'But Bassanio gave his ring away too,' said Gratiano. 'He gave his ring to the clever young judge. Then the boy, the judge's servant, wanted my ring. What could I do?'

Portia spoke angrily to Bassanio. 'You've broken your promise to me!' she cried. 'I'll never love you again!'

'You don't understand, Portia,' said Bassanio. 'I didn't want to give the ring to the judge, but I had to. He saved the life of my dearest friend. I offered him 3,000 gold pieces but he didn't want it. He only wanted this ring.'

'Please forgive Bassanio,' said Antonio. 'The young judge saved my life. I promise you that Bassanio will always be a good husband to you.'

'Then,' said Portia, taking out a ring, 'give him this ring. Tell him to look after it better than the other one.'

Bassanio looked at the ring. 'But it's the same ring!' he cried. 'I gave this ring to the young judge. I don't understand. What does this mean?'

'It means,' said Portia, 'that I was the young judge. And here's that young boy, my servant. It was Nerissa.'

Bassanio and Gratiano were very surprised. At first they couldn't speak. They couldn't believe Portia's story.

Portia had other news. She gave a letter to Antonio. In the letter was information about three of his ships. They weren't lost at sea; they were safe in Venice.

'This is wonderful news!' cried Antonio. 'Now I can live happily again!'

'It's almost morning,' said Portia. 'Let's go inside and talk there.'

'Yes,' said Gratiano. 'Come, young servant of the judge – or would you like to be my wife now?'

A Midsummer Night's Dream

A law existed in Greece which made young women very unhappy. By this law, a father was able to choose a man as a husband for his daughter. The daughter had to agree to marry this man, or die.

One day an old man, Egeus, came to the court of the Duke of Athens. Athens was the largest city in Greece and the duke was a very important man. Everybody in Athens did what he told them.

With Egeus were his beautiful young daughter, Hermia, and two young men. One of the young men was called Demetrius and the other was called Lysander.

'I've come to tell you about my daughter, Hermia,' Egeus said to the duke. He pointed to one of the young men. 'I've ordered her to marry this young man, Demetrius, but she refuses.' He pointed to the other young man. 'She says that she loves this young man, Lysander. But if she doesn't marry Demetrius, then by law she must die.'

'You must follow your father's orders, Hermia,' said the duke. 'Demetrius is a good man.'

'Lysander is a good man too,' answered Hermia.

Then Lysander spoke. 'I am as good and as rich as Demetrius,' he said. 'I love Hermia and she loves me. So why can't I marry her? I'll tell you something. In the past, Demetrius loved Hermia's friend, Helena, and she still loves him. So he should marry Helena.'

'I know,' said the duke. 'I've heard that too. But I can't change the laws of Athens. Hermia, you must do what your father wants. You must marry Demetrius, or die.'

◆

15

When Lysander and Hermia were alone, Lysander said, 'Listen to me, Hermia. I have an aunt who lives a long way from Athens. Let's go to her house and get married. The laws of Athens can't stop us there. Leave your father's house tomorrow night and meet me in the wood outside Athens. I'll wait for you there.'

'Yes, I'll meet you there,' replied Hermia. 'I promise!'

'Good, dear Hermia,' said Lysander. 'Keep your promise. Look, here comes Helena.'

'Beautiful Helena!' said Hermia. 'Where are you going?'

'Don't call me beautiful,' answered Helena sadly. 'I love Demetrius so much, but he loves you, not me. He loves your eyes, your voice and everything about you. Oh, teach me to copy your looks and your voice and I'll win his heart!'

'I don't want Demetrius to love me,' said Hermia. 'But he follows me all the time.'

'And I *do* want him to love *me*,' said Helena. 'But he hates me.'

'Don't be sad,' said Hermia. 'Demetrius won't see my face again. Tomorrow night, Lysander and I are going to leave Athens. We're going to meet in the wood outside the city. It's the wood where you and I have often met, dear Helena. And then I hope that you can have Demetrius.'

Later, when Helena was alone, she said to herself, 'Demetrius will never love me because he only loves Hermia. I'll go and tell him about her plan to leave Athens. Perhaps he'll be grateful to me because I told him. He'll follow her, and I can go with him.'

◆

The next night, Hermia and Lysander met in the wood outside Athens. They didn't know that many other people lived in the wood too. But these other people weren't ordinary people – they were fairies. The king and queen of the fairies were called Oberon and Titania.

But at that time Oberon and Titania weren't friends. Titania had a little servant boy, and Oberon wanted this boy as his servant. Titania didn't want to give the boy to Oberon, and so Oberon was very angry with her.

Titania was walking through the wood with her fairies. She didn't know that Oberon and his fairies were beginning their evening dances in the same part of the wood. It was a beautiful night and the moon was shining brightly.

When Oberon saw her, he said, 'This is an unlucky meeting on a lovely night. Why are you angry with me, Titania? I only want your servant boy.'

'Stop asking me for him!' replied Titania. 'The boy's mother is dead. She was a very good friend, and I'm keeping the boy because of her. I'll never give him to you. Come, fairies! We'll get angry if we stay here.'

Oberon wanted to make Titania sorry for her angry words. He called Puck, his favourite servant.

Puck was a very clever fairy. He was able to fly quickly to anywhere in the world. He loved to have fun. He was always thinking of new jokes to play on people.

'Listen, Puck,' said Oberon. 'I have an important job for you. There's a pretty flower called "Lazy Love". It has a very special kind of juice inside. When a man or woman is asleep, you can drop this magic juice on their eyes. After a time, they wake up. They fall in love with the first person or animal that they see. I showed that flower to you once – do you remember? Go and find it, and bring it to me now!'

'I'll go now,' said Puck. 'I'll fly round the world in forty minutes!'

He flew away quickly.

'While Titania is asleep,' thought Oberon, 'I'll drop some of the magic juice from the flower on her eyes. She'll fall in love with the first thing that she sees. She won't be interested in her little servant boy, and she'll give him to me.'

◆

17

While Puck was away, Demetrius and Helena passed through the wood near Oberon. Demetrius was following Hermia, but he didn't want Helena with him.

'Go away, Helena,' he said. 'I don't love you. I've come to this wood to find Hermia. I love her and I'm going to kill Lysander. So stop following me – I don't want you here.'

'But I love you,' answered Helena. 'I'll be like your dog. I'm going to follow you, Demetrius.'

'Then I'll run away from you,' said Demetrius. 'I'll leave you with the wild animals – perhaps they'll eat you.'

They walked through the wood without seeing the fairy king. But Oberon could see and hear everything. When he heard Demetrius's unkind words to Helena, he felt sad. He wanted to help her.

Then Puck returned with the flower.

Oberon took the flower and went to look for Titania. But before he left, he gave some of the juice from the flower to Puck.

'Take this magic juice and go through the wood,' he said. 'Look for a young man from Athens. A lovely lady is in love with him but he doesn't love her. Put some of the juice on his eyes when he's asleep. But watch him when he wakes up. The lady must be the first thing that he sees.'

'I'll do as you tell me,' said Puck, and he flew away.

Oberon found Titania asleep in a lovely place with many beautiful flowers. He dropped some of the magic juice on her eyes. His plan was going well and he was very pleased.

'When you wake up, the magic will work,' he said. 'You'll love the first thing that you see. So open your eyes when something ugly is near you!'

◆

While Oberon was putting the magic juice on Titania's eyes, Puck was looking for Demetrius and Helena. But he couldn't find them anywhere. He saw some workmen from Athens near Titania.

'What are these people doing here?' thought Puck. 'I'll stop and listen to them.'

The workmen were practising a play. They were planning to show the play at the wedding of the Duke of Athens. But the play wasn't going well. The workmen weren't good actors and they were saying a lot of stupid things.

The most stupid man was called Bottom. Puck decided to have some fun and to play a joke on Bottom. Soon Bottom left the others to practise his part in the play. So Puck followed and changed Bottom's head into the head of a donkey.

Bottom didn't know that he now had a donkey's head. But when he came back to the other workmen, they were afraid. They ran away. Bottom couldn't understand this.

'Why did they run away?' he thought. 'Perhaps they're trying to frighten me. But I'll show them that I'm not afraid. I'll stay here and I'll sing loudly.'

Bottom started to sing in his donkey's voice, and the loud noise woke Titania, the fairy queen. She opened her eyes. Bottom was the first person that she saw. The magic from the juice began to work and Titania fell deeply in love with the stupid workman with the donkey's head.

'Please sing again!' she said. 'You have a lovely voice. And you're so beautiful. Stay here with me. I love you!'

She called her four favourite fairies. 'Be kind and polite to this wonderful man,' she told them. 'Be his servants and help him. Look after him well. Bring him the best food.'

Then Titania and the fairies took Bottom to a very special part of the wood – her beautiful fairy garden.

'Come and sit with me on this bed of flowers,' she said to him. 'I shall put roses in your hair, and touch your lovely face and kiss your beautiful big ears.'

'Stay here with me. I love you!'

Bottom enjoyed having fairy servants. He told them to do a lot of stupid things. Titania agreed to everything. The magic was still working on her. She was in love with Bottom and she wanted to make him happy.

'What would you like to eat, my love?' she asked him.

'I want some dried grass,' replied Bottom. 'And then I'll go to sleep. Your people mustn't wake me.'

'Sleep in my arms,' said Titania. 'I love you so much!'

◆

After Puck gave Bottom the donkey's head, he continued to look for Helena and Demetrius. Finally, he saw a young man asleep in the wood. Near him was a beautiful young lady.

'Young men of Athens wear clothes like his clothes,' thought Puck. 'He's the man that Oberon told me about. Good. I'll put the juice on his eyes. The lady is very near him. He'll see her when he wakes up. Then he'll fall in love with her.'

Puck dropped some juice on to the man's eyes and flew back to Oberon. He was very pleased with his work.

But Puck made a mistake. The young man was Lysander, not Demetrius. The young lady was Hermia, not Helena!

Then Helena came to the place where Lysander and Hermia were sleeping. She was too tired to run after Demetrius now. So she was walking through the wood, sad and alone. She saw Lysander and woke him.

Lysander opened his eyes and the magic began to work. Suddenly he fell in love with the first person that he saw.

'Oh, Helena!' he cried. 'You're so beautiful! I'll run through fire for you! Where's that unkind Demetrius? I'll kill him.'

'Don't say that, Lysander,' said Helena. 'Demetrius loves your Hermia. But she loves you and you love her. Be happy about that.'

'No, no,' said Lysander. 'My time with Hermia was very boring. It's finished now. I love you, Helena.'

'Why are you laughing at me?' asked Helena sadly. 'I don't want to stay here and listen to you. I'm going.' She ran off into the wood again.

But Lysander really was in love with Helena now. Hermia was still asleep. So he left her and followed Helena into the wood.

Then Hermia woke up. She called out to Lysander, but he wasn't there. Hermia was alone and afraid. She ran into the wood to find him.

While Hermia was looking for Lysander, she met Demetrius in the wood. Demetrius was very pleased to see her. But Hermia wasn't pleased to see him.

◆

Puck went back to Oberon.

'Well?' asked Oberon. 'Did you put the love juice on the eyes of that unkind young man from Athens?'

'Yes,' replied Puck. 'Everything will be fine now. He'll see the lady when he wakes up. Then he'll fall in love with her.'

Then Puck and Oberon heard the voices of a man and a woman. The woman's voice was very angry.

'Look,' said Oberon. 'Here comes the young man.'

'The woman is the same,' said Puck, 'but the man is different. That's very strange.'

The two people were Hermia and Demetrius.

'Dear Hermia,' Demetrius was saying, 'why are you angry with me? I love you so much.'

'Where's my Lysander?' replied Hermia. 'Have you killed him? Kill me too. I don't want to live without him.'

'I don't know where he is,' said Demetrius.

'I don't believe you,' said Hermia. 'Did you kill him while he was asleep? That's very brave of you. I hate you!'

'You're wrong,' said Demetrius. 'I didn't kill him.'

But Hermia didn't believe Demetrius. She ran off into the wood. Demetrius was too tired to follow her, so he lay down on the ground. Soon he was asleep.

'What have you done?' Oberon said to Puck. 'You've made a terrible mistake. You've put the juice on the eyes of the wrong man. Go through the wood, find the other young lady and bring her here immediately. I'll put some juice on this man's eyes. Then he'll see her when he wakes up.'

◆

Puck soon found Helena. He brought her to the place where Demetrius was sleeping. She was followed by Lysander. He was still talking about his great love for her.

'Why are you laughing at me?' asked Helena sadly. 'Have you forgotten Hermia?'

'Hermia isn't important to me,' said Lysander. 'You're my only love, Helena.'

The sound of their voices woke Demetrius. He had the magic juice in his eyes. When he saw Helena, he fell in love with her. Now Lysander *and* Demetrius loved Helena.

'Helena!' Demetrius cried. 'You're so beautiful. Can I kiss you, my princess? I love you more than anything in the world.'

Helena couldn't understand what was happening.

'So now you both want to play games,' she said. 'Hate me if you like. But don't laugh at me.'

'Don't be unkind, Demetrius,' said Lysander. 'You love Hermia, not Helena. I'll give you Hermia. I don't love her now. I love Helena. I won't love another woman until I die.'

'You can keep Hermia!' shouted Demetrius. 'I'm not interested in her now. Helena is my only love!'

Hermia was still in the same part of the wood, and she heard the two men's voices. She came to see what was happening.

When she saw Lysander again, she was very happy.

'Lysander, dear Lysander!' she cried. 'Why did you leave me alone in the wood?'

'What do you want, Hermia?' asked Lysander. 'Go away. I don't love you now. I hate you. I love Helena.'

Hermia didn't believe him. But Helena said to her, 'I understand. The three of you – you and Lysander and Demetrius – have made a plan to hurt me. We've been good friends for many years, Hermia, and I loved you very much. How can you do this to me? How can you be so unkind?'

'I don't know what you mean,' said Hermia. She was getting angry too now. 'I don't understand. What's happening? Why is Lysander saying: "I love Helena now".'

'It's true!' shouted Lysander. 'I love you, Helena!'

'I love you more than him!' shouted Demetrius.

So the two men went off to another part of the wood to fight for Helena.

'I'm not staying here with you,' said Helena to Hermia. 'I'm going too.' She ran away, and Hermia followed her.

◆

'You did all this,' said Oberon to Puck.

'It was a mistake,' replied Puck. 'I looked for a young man from Athens and I dropped the magic juice on his eyes. That's what you told me to do. So I didn't do anything wrong. But I'm glad that I made a mistake. It's very funny!'

'And now,' said Oberon, 'we'll have to help these four young lovers. Listen to me.

'The two young men are looking for a place to fight. So fill the night with a thick black cloud. They won't be able to see through the cloud. They'll get tired and fall asleep.

'I have the juice from another flower here. Take it and put it on Lysander's eyes. His old love for Hermia will return. Demetrius will still be in love with Helena. So everyone will be happy again. Everything will seem like a dream. Go and do your work!'

◆

After Puck left, Oberon went to find Titania.

'I'll take the little boy from her,' he thought, 'and after that I'll make her free again. Then she'll stop loving that stupid man with the donkey's head.'

When Oberon found Titania, she was asleep. Her fairies and her servants lay near her. Oberon took the little servant boy from her.

Bottom lay near Titania with beautiful flowers round his head. He looked very stupid. Now Oberon began to feel sorry for his fairy queen. So he touched her eyes with another flower and Titania woke up.

'My Oberon!' cried Titania. 'I've had a very strange dream. I thought that I was in love with a donkey.'

'There he is,' replied Oberon, and pointed to Bottom.

'But how did this happen?' asked Titania. 'Oh, I can't look at his ugly face!'

Then Puck came back.

'Puck, take the donkey's head away from this man,' said Oberon. 'Titania, let's have some music. All these five people – Bottom, Demetrius, Lysander, Hermia and Helena – must fall into a deep sleep. When they wake up, they won't remember anything.'

'Let's have some music!' called Titania to her fairies.

'Come and dance with me, my queen,' said Oberon. 'Let's go round the world, faster than the moon.'

'Yes,' replied Titania. 'And you must tell me what happened. Why was I asleep near this donkey?'

Oberon and Titania left. They were good friends again, and very happy.

◆

Early the next morning, the Duke of Athens and Egeus, Hermia's father, came to the wood with their friends and servants. They were looking for the four young people, and found them asleep on the ground.

When they heard the voices of the duke and his friends, the young people woke up. They couldn't remember anything clearly. Everything was like a strange dream.

Lysander now loved Hermia, and Demetrius now loved Helena.

The duke was a very clever man. He saw that Demetrius didn't love Hermia now. He didn't know why. But he knew that this was a happy ending for everybody. Even Hermia's father, Egeus, had to agree with the duke. He couldn't order Hermia to marry Demetrius now.

'Let's all go back to Athens,' said the duke. 'There, Lysander will marry Hermia, and Demetrius will marry Helena. I too am getting married soon. Let's all get married and be happy!'

Hamlet

Hamlet was the Prince of Denmark. His father, the king, was dead. Two months after his death, Hamlet's mother, Gertrude, married Claudius, her dead husband's brother. Then Claudius became king.

Claudius was a bad man, but Gertrude didn't know this.

'Claudius always wanted to be king,' the people of Denmark said. 'Hamlet is the true king after his father's death. But Claudius didn't want that. That's why he married Queen Gertrude.'

Hamlet loved his dead father and he was very sad after his death. He became tired of the world and everything in it. He knew that there was something strange about his father's death. But he couldn't prove anything.

He was also very unhappy about his mother's marriage.

'How can my mother forget my dear father so quickly?' he thought. 'He loved her very much; he was a wonderful husband to her and an excellent father to me. But only two months after his death, she's married my uncle!'

Claudius tried many times to become friends with Hamlet. He wanted Hamlet to like him.

'Hamlet, you're like a son to me,' he said. 'Why are you still unhappy about your dead father? I'm your father now.'

'Don't think about your father so much,' Gertrude said to her son. 'Everybody has to die. Why do you look so sad? Why do you wear black clothes all the time?'

'I wear black clothes because I really am sad,' replied Hamlet. 'I can't forget my father quickly.'

◆

Hamlet had a good friend called Horatio. One day, Horatio came to Hamlet and told him a very strange story.

'I saw a ghost on the walls of the castle last night,' he said. 'The soldiers around the walls have seen it two or three times. They're very frightened. They told me about it, so last night I watched with them. I saw it too.'

'What ghost? What did it look like?' asked Hamlet.

'It looked like your dead father. I tried to speak to it, but it moved away. It didn't answer me.'

'Did you see its face?' asked Hamlet.

'Yes, I did. It looked . . . not angry, but very sad.'

'I'll watch with you tonight,' said Hamlet. 'Perhaps it will come again. I'll speak to it. I'll find out what it wants. I'll come to you on the walls between eleven and twelve. But don't say anything about this to anyone.'

After Horatio left, Hamlet thought for a long time. 'My father's ghost! Something's wrong. I'm sure that it wants to tell me something. When night comes, I'll know.'

That night, Hamlet joined Horatio and the soldiers who were guarding the walls. It was nearly midnight. Suddenly, Horatio looked up and cried out, 'There's the ghost!'

When he saw the ghost, Hamlet wasn't afraid. He spoke to it bravely: 'Tell me who you are. What do you want?'

The ghost looked at Hamlet. Then it held up its hand and pointed to a place away from the soldiers.

'It wants to speak to you alone,' cried Horatio. 'But don't go with it. Perhaps it will take you to a high place and throw you into the sea.'

But Hamlet wasn't afraid to follow the ghost. When he was alone with it, the ghost spoke to him.

'I'm your father's ghost,' it said. 'Listen to me, Hamlet. I was murdered by Claudius, your uncle. While I was asleep in my garden, Claudius poured poison into my ears. The poison went into my blood and killed me. But nobody could see the poison. Nobody knew how I died.

'This bad man, my brother, murdered me and then he married my wife, the queen. And now he's King of Denmark.

'You must do something, Hamlet. You must kill Claudius for his crime. But don't hurt your mother. Now, it's getting light and I have to leave you. Goodbye. But remember me.'

'You've told me terrible things,' said Hamlet. 'How can I forget you? I promise that I'll always remember you. My uncle is a very bad man. He smiles all the time, but inside, his heart is black.'

The ghost disappeared and Horatio came to Hamlet.

'Are you all right?' he asked. 'What did the ghost say?'

But Hamlet didn't want to tell Horatio everything.

'Promise me this,' he said to his friend. 'Don't tell anyone about tonight. Don't tell anyone about the ghost. And if I seem to act in a strange way, don't tell anyone the reason.'

Horatio didn't understand, but he promised.

◆

After he met the ghost, Hamlet changed. He pretended to be mad. He began to say and do very strange things. Everybody believed that he really was mad – even his mother, Gertrude. She became more and more worried about her son.

Hamlet was thinking all the time about the ghost. Did Claudius really kill his father? Was it possible to prove it?

Hamlet had two friends called Rosencrantz and Guildenstern. These two young men were at school with Hamlet. Now Claudius decided to send for them. He wanted them to find out what the problem was with Hamlet.

Hamlet was pleased at first to see his two friends. But then he asked them, 'Why did you come here? Did the king order you to see me?'

'Yes,' answered Rosencrantz and Guildenstern.

'I understand,' said Hamlet. 'The king's worried about me. I've changed a lot. I'm not happy now – I can't enjoy anything and I never laugh. Nothing in the world is interesting or beautiful – everything is ugly. Man is a wonderful thing – so clever and beautiful – but no man or woman can make me happy now.'

'Oh,' said Rosencrantz. 'But some actors are coming here to act in a play. You always enjoyed plays. Perhaps you'll like these actors, Hamlet.'

When the actors arrived, Hamlet welcomed them. Then he asked one of them to say a few words from a play. This play was about the death of an old king.

The actor told the story of the king very well. He explained how the old king was killed. The king's castle was burned. Then he spoke about the unhappy queen, the king's wife. The story was very sad, and the actor began to cry.

Hamlet saw this and thought, 'This actor is crying about a dead king in a story. But my father is really dead; he was murdered by my uncle. And what have I done about it? Nothing!'

Then Hamlet had an idea.

'I'll ask these actors to act a story which is like the death of my father. I'll ask Claudius to watch the play and I'll watch his face carefully. I want to be sure that the ghost was right. I want to be sure that Claudius murdered my father.'

◆

That evening, Hamlet met Horatio before the play and said, 'Watch my uncle's face carefully during the play.'

Then he went and sat next to Ophelia.

Ophelia was a lovely young girl who was Hamlet's girlfriend before his father's death. Her father, Polonius, was a servant of the king. Her brother, Laertes, was away in France.

After his father died, Hamlet could only think about his hate for his uncle. So he started to act very strangely towards Ophelia. Ophelia was very hurt. She loved Hamlet very much, but she couldn't understand the change in him. What was wrong with him? Why didn't he love her?

But at the play, Hamlet talked to Ophelia in a friendly way, and she was very surprised and pleased. Now he was like the old Hamlet again.

Claudius and Gertrude were at the play with all their friends. Hamlet and Horatio watched Claudius carefully.

The play began. Two actors played the parts of a king and queen. The queen in the play seemed to be very much in love with her husband. She said, 'If you die before me, I'll never marry again. Only women who kill their husbands marry a second time.'

The king then fell asleep in his garden. A relative of the king's entered and poured poison into the king's ears.

'Look!' cried Ophelia. 'Claudius is standing up!'

Claudius didn't want to watch the play. It showed too clearly how he killed his brother.

'What's the matter?' asked Gertrude.

'Stop the play!' shouted Polonius, Ophelia's father.

'Put the lights on!' cried Claudius. 'Go away, everybody! Leave the room!'

Claudius went out and everybody followed him. Hamlet and Horatio were left alone.

'Did you see what the king did, Horatio?' asked Hamlet. 'Now I'm sure that he killed my father.'

One of the queen's servants came to Hamlet and asked him to go to the queen's room. The queen wanted to talk to him.

Ophelia's father, Polonius, was hiding behind a curtain in the queen's room. He wanted to listen to Hamlet's words to his mother. Then he could tell Claudius. Gertrude knew that Polonius was behind the curtain. But Hamlet didn't know that he was there.

Hamlet went into the queen's room. 'What's the matter, mother?' he asked.

31

'You've made your father very angry,' replied Gertrude.

'My father! But Claudius isn't my father. You did a terrible thing to my father,' replied Hamlet.

'Don't speak to me like that, Hamlet,' said Gertrude. 'Have you forgotten who I am?'

'No. You're the queen, the wife of your husband's brother. Sit down. I'm going to tell you about yourself.'

The queen was afraid of Hamlet. 'What are you going to do?' she asked. 'Are you going to kill me?' Then she cried, 'Help! Help!'

From behind the curtain, Polonius heard the queen's cries. He began to shout too: 'Help! Help!'

'What is it?' cried Hamlet. 'Who's there?' He thought that it was Claudius. So he took out his sword and pushed it through the curtain. It went into Polonius.

'You've killed me!' said Polonius, and died.

Hamlet pulled back the curtain and saw Polonius.

'Don't speak to me like that Hamlet,' said Gertrude.

32

' *You've* done a terrible thing, Hamlet,' said the queen. 'You've killed Polonius.'

'Yes,' said Hamlet. 'I've done a terrible thing. It's almost as bad as the murder of a king and marriage to his brother.'

'What!' said the queen. 'The murder of a king?'

'Yes,' replied Hamlet. 'What's the matter with you, mother? My father was an excellent man. How could you forget about him so quickly, and marry someone like my uncle? Were you crazy? Why did you do it?'

'Stop! That's enough!' said the queen.

But Hamlet didn't stop. He was getting angrier and angrier.

'He's a very bad man,' he said. 'A murderer who . . .'

Suddenly the ghost came into the room. Hamlet saw it and stopped.

'What do you want?' Hamlet asked it. 'I haven't forgotten my promise to you. I'm going to kill Claudius.'

'Who are you talking to?' said Gertrude. 'Are you mad?'

'Good,' said the ghost. 'But look at your mother, Hamlet. She's very frightened. Speak to her.'

'What's the matter with you, mother?' asked Hamlet.

'What's the matter with *you*, Hamlet?' replied Gertrude. 'You're looking at nothing and talking to the air. What can you see?'

'*Him*, mother! Can't you see him too?'

'What do you mean, Hamlet? I can't see anything!'

'It's the ghost of my father!' cried Hamlet. 'Look there. He's wearing the same clothes as he always did. Now he's going away.'

'What are you talking about?' said Gertrude. 'There's no ghost. You're imagining it. You're mad.'

'I'm not mad. My father's ghost has come here because of your crime. Oh, mother, please don't go back to Claudius.'

'Hamlet, you've broken my heart,' said Gertrude sadly and left the room.

♦

Claudius saw Gertrude later. He knew immediately that something was wrong.

'How's Hamlet?' he asked her.

'He's completely mad,' replied Gertrude. 'He's as mad as the wind and sea when they fight. He heard something move behind the curtain in my room. Then he took out his sword and killed that good old man, Polonius.'

'This mad young prince is dangerous,' said Claudius. 'We must send him away immediately.'

Then he had an idea. He wanted to kill Hamlet, but he couldn't kill him in Denmark. People loved Hamlet very much. So Claudius thought of a plan. He wrote a letter to the King of England. Then he sent for Hamlet's two friends, Rosencrantz and Guildenstern.

'I'm sending Hamlet to England tonight,' he told them. 'You're his old friends and I want you to go with him on the ship. Take this letter with you. When you arrive, give it to the King of England.'

In the letter, Claudius asked the King of England to kill Hamlet immediately. He told Rosencrantz and Guildenstern about his plan. Now they knew what was in the letter. But they still agreed to take it to the King of England.

Then Claudius ordered Hamlet to come to him.

'I'm sending you to England,' he said. 'When the people of Denmark hear about Polonius's murder, they'll be very angry. Perhaps they'll try to kill you. But you'll be safe in England. Get ready quickly – a ship is waiting to take you.'

♦

While he was at sea, Hamlet thought a lot about Claudius. He was sure that Claudius was planning something bad. One night he couldn't sleep, so he got up. He found the letter that Rosencrantz and Guildenstern were taking to the King of England.

Hamlet opened the letter and read it.

'So Claudius has told the King of England to kill me,' he thought. 'And Rosencrantz and Guildenstern knew about this. They're not good friends to me – they're my enemies.'

Then he had an idea. He changed the name of 'Hamlet' in the letter to 'Rosencrantz and Guildenstern.' He closed the letter again. He was very pleased with himself.

The next day, the ship was attacked by enemy sailors. During the fight, Hamlet jumped on to the enemy ship. While he was there, his ship escaped.

The sailors discovered that Hamlet was a prince. They were very kind to him after that. He promised to help them later, and they took him back to Denmark.

◆

Hamlet was returning to his uncle's palace when he met his good friend Horatio. As they walked on their way, they saw two men near a church. They were making a large hole in the ground.

'Who's this for?' Hamlet asked. 'Who's died?'

But the men didn't tell him.

Then Hamlet saw a lot of people coming towards the church. Claudius and Gertrude were there with their friends and servants. A young man was there too. When he saw the young man, Hamlet was very surprised.

'That's Laertes, Ophelia's brother,' thought Hamlet. 'What's he doing here? He was away in France. Why has he come back to Denmark? Who's died?'

People were carrying the dead body of a young girl. When Hamlet saw the body, he couldn't believe his eyes.

'That's Ophelia!' said Hamlet. He felt very sad.

Ophelia loved Hamlet very much. When Hamlet killed

Polonius, her father, her heart was broken. She went mad. She started singing strange songs all the time, and picking flowers in the fields and woods.

One day, she tried to get some flowers from a tree by the river. As she was climbing the tree, she fell into the river. Her heavy clothes pulled her under the water and she died.

When Laertes heard the news of his father's death, he came back to Denmark from France. He found his sister mad and soon after that she died. So now Laertes was very sad and angry. He hated Hamlet. He wanted to kill the prince.

Ophelia's body was put into the ground. Then Queen Gertrude threw some flowers down on to the body.

'Here are some lovely flowers for a lovely lady,' she said sadly. 'I wanted to give you flowers on the day of your marriage to my son, not for your death.'

Suddenly Laertes jumped down into the hole.

'Don't throw any earth down yet,' he cried. 'I want to hold my dear sister in my arms again!'

Hamlet ran and jumped down into the hole with Laertes. Everybody was very surprised to see him.

'Hamlet!' cried the queen. 'What are you doing here?'

'I loved Ophelia very much,' said Hamlet. 'I loved her more than Laertes – more than 40,000 brothers!'

When Laertes saw Hamlet, he began to fight him.

'Stop!' cried Gertrude. 'Don't fight him!'

'Leave him, Laertes,' said Claudius. 'He's mad.'

The king's servants stopped the two angry young men and pulled them out of the hole.

◆

Later, Claudius and Laertes discussed a plan to kill Hamlet.

Laertes was very good with his sword. He planned to fight Hamlet and kill him in this way. But Hamlet was also good at swordfighting.

'I want to be sure that I'll kill Hamlet,' said Laertes to Claudius. 'I'll choose a sharp sword, and I'll put poison on the end. If it touches Hamlet, he'll die.'

'Excellent!' said Claudius. 'But I want to be sure of his death, so I'll do something too. During the fight, I'll offer him a drink of wine. But the wine will have poison in it.'

Claudius and Laertes thought that they were very clever. But everything went wrong.

◆

When Hamlet and Laertes met for the fight, everybody came to watch them – the king, the queen, Horatio and all their other friends.

The fight was in a large room. At one end, near the king and queen, was a table with cups of wine on it. Before the fight, Hamlet spoke to Laertes. He wanted to be friends.

'Please forgive me,' he said. 'I know that I've acted very badly. But I was mad. I'm very sorry – I didn't want to hurt you. I love you like my brother.'

'I accept what you say,' said Laertes. 'But we must still fight.'

The fight began. At first, Hamlet was winning. Claudius offered him a drink from the cup of poisoned wine. But Hamlet wasn't thirsty and didn't want a drink.

'I'll drink it later,' he said.

Claudius put the cup down. Before he could stop her, the queen picked it up. She drank from it and was poisoned.

The two young men were still fighting. Then Laertes cut Hamlet with his poisoned sword. A few minutes later, both men dropped their swords. By mistake, Hamlet picked up Laertes sword. Then he cut Laertes with it. So now both men were hurt with the poisoned sword.

Suddenly, the queen fell to the floor.

'Mother!' shouted Hamlet. 'What's the matter?'

'She feels ill. She doesn't like to see the blood,' said Claudius.

The fight began. At first, Hamlet was winning.

But the queen cried out, 'No, no! It's the drink! The drink!
It's poisoned!'

Then Laertes fell.

'Hamlet!' he cried. 'My sword was poisoned. We're both
going to die. Your mother drank a cup of poison too. The king
did all this.'

'Poisoned sword?' said Hamlet. 'Good. Here's the best place
for it!' He ran towards Claudius and pushed the sword into
Claudius's heart. Then he took the cup of poison and ordered
Claudius to drink from it. The king fell dead.

'Forgive me, Hamlet!' said Laertes. 'The king mixed that
poison. He killed my father and me, not you!'

Laertes died.

Hamlet knew that he was dying too. He turned to his best
friend, Horatio.

'Horatio,' he said, 'I'm dying. But you're still alive. You must tell my story to the world.'

'There's still some poison in the cup,' said Horatio. 'I don't want to live. I shall drink the poison and die with you.'

'No, Horatio,' said Hamlet. 'If you really love me, help me. Tell everybody my story.'

Then Hamlet died.

'Now an excellent man is dead,' said Horatio sadly. 'Goodbye, my dear prince!'

Horatio didn't drink the poison. He told the sad and terrible story of Hamlet, Prince of Denmark, to the world.

Julius Caesar

About 2,000 years ago, a great man called Julius Caesar was the ruler of Rome. He was a wise man, and he ruled Rome well. He had great power, but after some time he wanted more.

There were two important Romans, Brutus and Cassius, who were worried about Caesar. They thought that he had too much power.

'Caesar's only a man, like us,' said Cassius to Brutus one day. 'He's not special, like a king. Why does he act like a king in front of the people of Rome?'

Brutus was a good friend of Caesar's, but he was worried too. 'I love Caesar,' he replied, 'but I don't want him to be king. The people want it, but he'll have too much power. That's not good for Rome.'

Caesar's best friend was called Mark Antony. Caesar saw Cassius talking to Brutus. He said to Antony, 'What are those two talking about? I don't like Cassius – he has a thin, hungry kind of look. He's always watching me and he never smiles. He's a dangerous man.'

'Don't be afraid of Cassius, Caesar,' replied Antony. 'He's a good Roman.'

'I'm not afraid of him,' said Caesar. 'I'm not afraid of anyone or anything, because I'm Caesar.'

◆

That night there was a great storm in the city of Rome. Many strange and terrible things were seen. Wild animals ran through the streets of the city, but they didn't attack anyone. There were men in the streets of Rome who were on fire. The old men of the city knew that something terrible was happening.

Brutus couldn't sleep. He was walking in his garden, still very unhappy about Caesar. He thought for a long time about his talk with Cassius. Finally he decided.

'Caesar must die,' he thought. 'He isn't my enemy as a man. But if he becomes king, he'll change. He'll become dangerous to Rome. So it's better for everybody if he dies. There's no other way.'

A servant, Lucius, came to find Brutus. He held a piece of paper in his hand.

'Sir,' said Lucius, 'I found this letter near the window. It wasn't there when I went to bed.'

Brutus took the letter and read these words:

Brutus, you are asleep. Wake up and look at yourself.
Is it right for one man alone to rule Rome? Do something about it!

When Brutus finished reading the letter, Lucius said, 'Sir, Cassius and some other men are at the door. They're waiting to speak to you. But I don't know who the other men are. They've pulled their hats over their faces.'

Brutus knew the men and welcomed them into his house. He knew that they were planning Caesar's death. But Cassius wasn't sure about Brutus. Brutus, he knew, was a very important man and a good friend of Caesar.

Cassius spoke alone to Brutus for some time. Finally Brutus decided to help with Cassius's plan to kill Caesar. He shook hands with each of the men.

'We must kill Caesar's friend, Mark Antony, too,' said Cassius. 'If we kill Caesar, perhaps he'll be dangerous. Let's kill him while we can. Antony and Caesar will die together. Then Antony won't be a problem for us later.'

'No,' said Brutus. 'We only need to kill Caesar. If we cut off a man's head, that's enough. He's dead then. We don't need to cut off his arms and legs too. Antony is only an arm of Caesar. Also, we want people to understand the reason for Caesar's death. It's for Rome – not because we want to murder everybody.'

'But I'm afraid of Mark Antony,' said Cassius. 'He's very clever and he really loves Caesar.'

'Don't think about him,' replied Brutus. 'If he loves Caesar so much, perhaps he'll kill himself after Caesar's death.'

◆

The next morning, Caesar's wife, Calpurnia, was very frightened.

'Please don't go out today, Caesar,' she said. 'Stay at home. Last night I had a very bad dream. I dreamt that someone was killing you. And terrible things are happening in the city. I don't understand them, but I'm afraid. If you go out, perhaps something bad will happen to you.'

'All right, dear Calpurnia,' said Caesar, 'I'll stay at home. Mark Antony can do my work today.'

Then Decius, a friend of Cassius, arrived. 'Are you ready to go out, Caesar?' he asked. 'The people are waiting for you.'

Decius was part of the group that was planning Caesar's death. He wanted to make sure that Caesar left his house that day.

'I'm not going out today,' replied Caesar. 'My wife has asked me to stay at home. She had a bad dream last night and she's afraid for my life.'

'But you can't stay at home today, Caesar,' said Decius. 'The people are planning to make you king. If you don't come, perhaps they'll change their minds. And everyone will laugh at you because you listen to your wife's dreams. They'll say, "Caesar is afraid."'

'You're right, Decius,' said Caesar. 'It *is* silly to listen to Calpurnia. Let's go!'

So Caesar went with Decius to the great building where all the important men of Rome met. Every day they went there to discuss important matters.

Brutus and Cassius and their friends were waiting for Caesar. They watched him go into the building. Mark Antony was there too.

'Good morning, everybody,' said Caesar. 'You're here very early today.'

As Caesar went inside, Brutus said to the other men, 'We must get as close as possible to Caesar. Metullus, Caesar sent your brother away from Rome. Ask him to bring your brother back. Then, while Caesar is talking to you, we can kill him.'

At the same time, another man in the group stopped Mark Antony and began to talk to him. So Antony didn't notice what was happening to Caesar.

Metullus stood in front of Caesar. 'Great Caesar,' he began, 'please will you change your mind about my brother?'

'Other people change their minds,' replied Caesar. 'But not me. I'm the great Caesar.'

'Please, Caesar . . .'

But before Metullus could finish, Cassius and the other men ran towards Caesar. They began to push their knives into him. Soon the ground was red with Caesar's blood.

But Caesar didn't die immediately.

Brutus came to join the others. He pushed his knife into Caesar. Caesar looked at him sadly, and said, 'You too, Brutus?'

Then at last Caesar fell to the ground and died.

◆

Antony couldn't help Caesar. So when Caesar died, Antony went home. Later, he sent his servant to Brutus.

'I've come from Mark Antony,' the servant said. 'He wants to know the reason why Caesar was killed.'

'Mark Antony is a good and wise man,' answered Brutus. 'Ask him to come here. We'll tell him why Caesar died. I promise that he'll return home safely.'

43

'I'm the great Caesar'

While they waited for Mark Antony, Brutus said, 'I know that Antony will be a good friend to us.'

'I'm afraid of him,' said Cassius. 'We must be careful.'

When Mark Antony arrived, he said to Brutus and his friends, 'I don't know what you're planning now. If you want to kill me, do it. Do it with the swords that are red with Caesar's blood.'

'Oh, Antony,' cried Brutus, 'we don't want to lift our swords against you. You can only see our hands with blood on them; you can't see our sad hearts. We killed Caesar because it was better for Rome. We love you like a brother.

'Wait until we've spoken to the people. Then you'll learn why I did this. I killed Caesar, but I loved him.'

'Let me shake hands with you all,' replied Mark Antony. 'I'm sure that you're very wise. I love you all and I agree with you. But I want to know: Why was Caesar dangerous for Rome?

'I also want to ask you for something: Give me your permission to show his body to the people. I, as his best friend, will tell them what was good about him.'

Cassius didn't like this idea. 'Don't agree to this, Brutus,' he said. 'Don't give Mark Antony permission to talk to the people. He's dangerous.'

'There won't be any problem,' Brutus replied. 'What can he say to hurt us? I'll speak first. I'll tell the crowd why we killed Caesar. He can speak after me.'

'I still don't like it,' said Cassius.

Brutus and his friends left Mark Antony alone with the dead body of Caesar.

After they left, Mark Antony looked sadly at the body of the great man.

He said, 'Forgive me, Caesar; I had to be nice to these men. You were the best and greatest man who ever lived. I'm going to destroy the men who did this terrible thing to you. There will be a long war and a lot of people will die. I promise you something. I won't rest until Brutus and Cassius and their friends are dead.'

Then a servant arrived. He was the servant of Octavius Caesar, the son of Julius Caesar's brother. Octavius was a few miles outside the city. He planned to visit his uncle, and didn't know about his death.

The servant saw Caesar's dead body and his eyes filled with tears.

'Go back to Octavius,' Antony said to him. 'Tell him what's happened. Rome isn't safe for him now. No, wait. Don't go back until I've spoken to the people tomorrow. Then you can tell Octavius how they feel.'

◆

The next day, a large crowd came to listen to Brutus. Brutus was a very good speaker. He knew how to talk to the crowd.

'I loved Caesar very much,' he said. 'But I had to kill him because I loved Rome more. Caesar wanted too much power. Did you want him to live and make you all his servants? Or is it better that Caesar is dead? Now you can live as free men.

'I love Rome more than anything. I'll kill myself if it helps Rome. I'll do it with the same knife that killed Caesar.'

As Brutus finished speaking, Mark Antony and his servants arrived. They were carrying Caesar's body.

The people liked Brutus's words very much. They agreed with him and shouted, 'Brutus must take Caesar's place!'

Brutus didn't want this, so he said, 'Good people, I'm going home now. But please stay and listen to Antony. We've given him permission to speak to you about Caesar. Stay here and listen to him.'

'All right,' said one man. 'He can speak. But he mustn't say anything against Brutus.'

'That Caesar was a terrible man,' said another man.

'Yes,' said another. 'It's a good thing that he's dead.'

'Silence!' said the first man. 'Let's listen to Antony.'

Mark Antony began to speak.

'Friends, Romans, . . . listen to me. A man's bad actions live after him; his good actions often die with him. But Caesar was a great man and my very good friend. He was a good friend to Rome too. He did many things for you. He brought a lot of money to the city. When the poor people cried, Caesar cried too.

'Brutus says: "Caesar wanted more power." But I asked Caesar to be king three times in the past. You all heard me. And three times he refused to be king. But we must believe what Brutus says. We must believe him because Brutus is an excellent man.

'You all loved Caesar. You were right to love him. So why don't you feel sorry about his death now?'

The people in the crowd began to talk.

'Antony's right,' said one man. 'We've been unkind to Caesar.'

'Antony is the finest man in Rome,' said another man. 'Look! His eyes are red from crying.'

'Yesterday,' continued Antony, 'Caesar was the greatest man in the world. Now look at him. He lies there and nobody feels sorry about his death. We should be very angry with Brutus and Cassius. But as you know, they're excellent men. So I don't want to say anything bad about them.

'I have a paper here – Caesar's will. He wrote it some time ago. It says what will happen to his money and his land after his death. But I won't read it to you. If I read it to you, you'll be very grateful to Caesar.'

'Read it to us, Antony,' shouted one man. 'We want to hear Caesar's will!'

Then everybody shouted, 'Read the will, Antony! We want to hear it!'

'I can't read it. I don't want to hurt those excellent men who killed Caesar. I can't read it.'

'Yes, Antony, yes! Read the will!'

'I have a paper here – Caesar's will.'

'All right,' said Antony at last. 'Come and stand around Caesar's body. Look down at him. See, this is the hole which Cassius's knife made. And here is where the excellent Brutus cut him with his sword. That was the unkindest cut of all. Caesar loved Brutus very much. When he saw Brutus, great Caesar's heart broke. Then he fell, and his blood ran everywhere.

'Now you're crying for him, good people. But you've forgotten Caesar's will. Listen. Caesar has left money to every Roman. He's left you all his private gardens to walk and play in. I'm telling you – there will never be a great man like Caesar again!'

The people were all very excited and angry now.

'Let's kill those bad men, Brutus and Cassius, and their friends!' they shouted. 'Let's burn down their houses!'

Then they carried away Caesar's body and Antony was left alone.

'Good,' he thought. 'I've started something. Let's see what happens now.'

Later, a servant came to him.

'Octavius has just arrived in Rome,' he said. 'And Brutus and Cassius have left the city.'

Antony met Octavius and they talked for a long time. They decided to join together to kill Brutus and Cassius and all Caesar's other enemies.

◆

Brutus realized too late that Mark Antony was very clever and very dangerous. When he spoke after Caesar's death, he turned many people against Brutus and Cassius.

Brutus and Cassius knew that they had to fight. They took their soldiers up into the hills outside Rome. There they prepared to fight Mark Antony. But Antony was in a very strong position. Octavius was helping him, and Octavius had many more soldiers than Brutus and Cassius.

Brutus and Cassius couldn't agree about the best place to

fight. They were still up in the hills with their soldiers. Down below them was a place called Philippi. Octavius and Antony were travelling towards this place.

'Let's go down to Philippi immediately and meet the enemy there,' said Brutus.

'No,' replied Cassius. 'Let's stay here up in the hills. It will be better if the enemy has to look for us. Then their soldiers will be tired when they fight against us.'

'The people between here and Philippi are our enemies,' said Brutus. 'If Antony comes up here, they'll join his soldiers. If we stay here, they'll find us in a very weak position. Now our soldiers are strong. Let's go down to Philippi and fight Antony there.'

Cassius was silent. Finally he agreed to go to Philippi.

After Cassius left, Brutus stayed in his tent. But he couldn't sleep. He tried to read, but suddenly he saw a strange and terrible shape before him. He jumped up in fear.

'Who are you?' he cried. 'What do you want?'

'I'm Caesar's ghost,' replied the shape. 'I've come to tell you something. You'll see me again at Philippi.'

Then the ghost disappeared.

◆

Antony, Octavius and their soldiers were waiting at Philippi.

'Look', said Octavius, 'The enemy are coming down from the hills.'

'Yes,' replied Antony. 'They want to show us that they're not afraid. But they're making a mistake.'

Cassius was preparing himself for the fight, but he wasn't happy. That morning he saw a very bad sign. Large black birds began to fly above the soldiers' heads and look down on them. They were looking for dead men to eat.

'If we lose this fight,' Cassius said to Brutus, 'will you go back to Rome as Antony's prisoner?'

50

'Never,' replied Brutus. 'Today must end the work that began with Caesar's death. But I don't know how things will end. I don't know if we'll meet again.

'So let's say goodbye for ever, Cassius. If we meet again, we'll laugh about all this. And if we don't meet again – we said goodbye.'

'You're right, Brutus,' said Cassius. 'Let's say goodbye now.'

◆

The fight began soon after that. At one time, it seemed that Brutus was winning, At another time, it seemed that Antony and Octavius were winning.

Brutus and Cassius were fighting in different places. Finally, Cassius's soldiers began to fall back. Antony's soldiers began to burn the tents of Cassius's soldiers.

Cassius saw that the fight was lost. He called one of his soldiers and gave him his sword. Then he asked the man to kill him with it. Sadly, the soldier did this, and then he went to find Brutus.

When Brutus saw Cassius's dead body, he was very sad about the death of his brave friend. He looked at the sword in Cassius's heart, and remembered the ghost of Caesar. He too knew that the fight was lost.

'You're still stronger than us, Caesar,' he said.

The fight continued, and all Brutus's friends were killed. Now the enemy were coming closer and closer. But Brutus, like Cassius, was a very brave man. He didn't think about running away. He preferred to die.

Brutus took out his sword. He ordered a soldier to hold it out. Then he threw himself on it.

'Caesar, now you can be happy,' he cried, as he died. 'I want to kill myself more than I wanted to kill you.'

When the fight finally ended, Mark Antony and Octavius looked down at Brutus's dead body.

'This was the finest Roman of them all,' said Antony sadly. 'The others only wanted Caesar's power. But Brutus thought about the good of the people. He really was a great man.'

ACTIVITIES

The Merchant of Venice

Before you read

1 Find these words in your dictionary:

duke   flesh   lead   merchant   mercy   pretend   servant

  a Which are words for people?
  b Which word means:
   (i) a heavy metal?
   (ii) the meat of an animal or person?
  c What are the other words in your language?

2 Read the beginning of the Introduction to the book. Who are the most important people in the story? What do you know about them?

After you read

3 Which of these five people in the story – Antonio, Bassanio, Shylock, Portia and Nerissa –
  a live in Venice?   **b** put on different clothes?
  c lend money?   **d** chooses something wisely?
  e give their husband a ring?   **f** wants a pound of flesh?

4 Answer these questions.
  a Why can't Antonio pay Shylock?
  b What must Shylock *not* take from Antonio?
  c Why doesn't Bassanio want to give the judge his ring?

A Midsummer Night's Dream

Before you read

5 Discuss these questions.
  a Do you ever dream? Can you remember what your dreams are about?
  b Why is a dream a good subject for a play?

6 Answer the questions. Check the meanings of the words in *italics* in your dictionary.

    a What does a *donkey* look like?

    b Do you believe in *fairies*?

    c What does *magic* do?

    d Are *midsummer* days long or short?

After you read

  7 Are these sentences correct or not? If not, correct them.

    a Hermia's father wants her to marry Lysander.

    b Titania wants to take the little boy from Oberon.

    c Puck puts the flower juice onto Bottom's eyes.

    d When the four lovers wake up, Demetrius is still in love with Helena.

  8 You are Bottom. What happened to you? Tell your friends.

Hamlet

Before you read

  9 *Hamlet* is one of Shakespeare's greatest plays. What do you know about the story?

10 Find these words in your dictionary:

    castle curtain ghost mad poison sword

    Complete this story.

    Last year I visited an old .... I saw the .... of an old man there behind a .... in one of the bedrooms. The man was .... He put .... in his wife's food and then killed himself with his ....

After you read

11 What are these people's names?

    a Hamlet's girlfriend   **b** Hamlet's mother

    c Ophelia's brother   **d** Gertrude's husband

    e Hamlet's best friend   **f** Ophelia's father

12 In *Hamlet*, death comes to Polonius, Ophelia, Gertrude, Laertes, Claudius and Hamlet. Which of these deaths is the saddest, do you think?